WHITE SEA

White Sea

POEMS
Cleopatra Mathis

Sarabande  Books

LOUISVILLE, KENTUCKY

No part of this book may be reproduced without written permission
of the publisher. Please direct inquiries to:

Managing Editor
Sarabande Books, Inc.
2234 Dundee Road, Suite 200
Louisville, KY 40205

Library of Congress Cataloging-in-Publication Data

Mathis, Cleopatra, 1947–
White sea : poems / by Cleopatra Mathis.— 1st ed.
p.   cm.
ISBN 1-932511-16-4 (hardcover : alk. paper)
— ISBN 1-932511-17-2 (pbk. : alk. paper)
I. Title.
PS3563.A8363W48 2005
811'.54—dc22
2004020569

13-digit ISBN 978-1-932-51116-1 (hc); 978-1-932-51117-8 (pb)

Cover image: *Sun Path* by Pat de Groot
Provided courtesy of the artist

Cover and text design by Charles Casey Martin

Manufactured in Canada
This book is printed on acid-free paper.

Sarabande Books is a nonprofit literary organization.

Partial funding has been provided by the Kentucky Arts Council,
a state agency in the Commerce Cabinet, with support from
the National Endowment for the Arts.

FIRST EDITION

For Stanley Kunitz

And to the memory of Linda Corrente, 1953–1999

TABLE OF CONTENTS

ACKNOWLEDGMENTS

I would like to thank the magazines and journals that first published these poems, sometimes in an earlier version:

Crying Sky: "The Old Question" (as "Hermit Thrush") and
        "The Herring Run" (as "On the Cape")
Louisiana Literature: "The Source"
The Marlboro Review: "White Morning" and "Again, Autumn"
        (as "Lesson")
Ms: "Salt"
The New Yorker: "Cane" and "Stanley's First Death"
Rattapallax: "Soul" (as "More about the Soul")
Rivendell Magazine: "Envoy"
River Styx: "Stanley and Elise"
Shenandoah: "The Release, Part II" (as "Threnody, After Six
       Months") and "Want"
Sou'wester: "Same Old," "Speech to the Self," and "Called
       Back, Part I"
The Southern Review: "At Boris's on the Outer Beach,"
       "Burial," and the second section of
       "Stanley's First Death" (as "Faithful")
The Threepenny Review: "Death of a Gull"
Tryst: "Listen, Spirit," "White Sea," "Vulture, Circling" and
       "You Wouldn't Say Goodbye"
U.S. 1 Worksheets: "Death of Puzzle"
The Worcester Review: "Stanley's Farewell"

"Willful" (as "Ars Poetica") was published in *The Gift of Light: for Donald Sheehan.*

"Willful" (as "Ars Poetica") was published in *The Gift of Light: for Donald Sheehan.*

All my thanks and praise to the Corporation of Yaddo, which gave me the gift of time and solace to write these poems, and to both the Outer Cape Artist's Residency Consortium and Peaked Hill Trust for residencies in the Margo-Gelb shack on the outer beach of the Cape Cod National Seashore. Also I am grateful to the National Endowment for the Arts for a fellowship that aided the completion of this book and to Dartmouth College for the support of the Curtis Welling Grant. And to the Fine Arts Work Center in Provincetown, Massachusetts, I owe a continuing debt.

My deepest appreciation goes to the friends who are closest to this book and offered invaluable help, especially Pamela Harrison, Ellen Bryant Voigt, Allison Funk, and Martha Webster. Special thanks, also, to Sarah Gorham and Jeffrey Skinner at Sarabande.

WHITE SEA

SALT

All those years I went the way of grief,
    turning my stony eye on disorder, something to be cleaned
        and fixed. I was lost, scrubbing away at the hidden,

hating the vase where the fruit flies nested,
    the artful bowl that held ruined fruit.
        Throw away the rot, I said, making myself saint

of the immaculate, not knowing a thing about the soul.
    Meanwhile, little spirit, essence, psyche, anima,
        the forever-alive-but-unpinnable one

turned its gaze away, claimed a crack,
    found a rusty needle, curled up in the eye of it.
        In the pine floors alone, a million crevices,

a million particles of grit, pinch, and crumb.
    What sea in my bucket could wash the world clean?
        And who knew the soul

was right at home in dust, passing
    through every incarnation: the tiny breathing
        mite it entered in the gray swirl under the stove,

expelling itself into a draft that carried it
    into the filmy grease so lightly pocked
        on the cabinet glass. Releasing, floating down,

the soul finding the one grain of salt
    lying there under my nose. Me at the sink,
        scouring the porcelain, not seeing.

I

THE SOURCE

Morning arrives in Louisiana, green going sour
with heat. Against the screen, oleander
scrapes its thicket of blooms,

cardinals gather in the yard, too many to count
with their rough voices, the single abrupt chirp.
My grandfather will not touch those birds,

though he shoots others with a stone and sling
and stews them whole,
nested in onion broth with whole garlic and clove.

Plain brown wrens, song sparrows—for him
no different from the figs he picks into his hat.
I hide in the Muscadine vines

pretending to play. He can't speak English
and I won't speak Greek. I can hear him calling,
each word hitting its mark,

and so I go to him with all my refusal.
From the blushing spot on each blossom end,
he peels back the skin for the fig's red meat,

he slips the coarse black covers off the grapes
and feeds me in the shade. It's too hot.
I lick the skin on my forearm. He's talking,

telling me that taste is like the sea.
I have never seen the sea. He's in another country
trying to tell me something. I look away.

COTTON

Blind to the back-lit
sheen of blackest black,
a dozen browns, even the muddy gold
a shadowed step from my own olive cast,
I played at cotton picking. Out there in the field,
ready bouquets spangled the row's
sparse scraggle. It was a contradiction,
those soft lights in the tableau of raw dirt,
rags and skin under the sun's flat whip at noon.
By then, I dragged my sack along with the dream
the school text showed: singing pickers,
one common black against the shock of white
bursting from the weightless burlap bags.
                        It was a lesson in not-thinking.
I got as far as *bad luck, born black,*
though from a distance my uncle gleamed
dark as coffee against his velvet Harley
riding in to take me home. Not far enough
for my fingers to bleed from the stubborn bolls,
my bent back aching to straighten.
Every sin forgotten
for the sake of that unlikely bud, innocent staple,
the future cloth on all our backs.
But before the machinery separated the black
tenacious seeds from the white,
I studied a fistful. It was a cloud in my pocket.

I fingered the billowy puff until it knotted
into a dull wad, nothing I could recognize.

THE WAITING

Not my climbers: black gum, sour gum, oak,
not the silvery underside of the dear mimosa
where I spent hours reading, but Louisiana's tree,

green through every season. Under the magnolia,
on my back, knees bent, bare feet flat on the dirt,
I gazed at my hands, already my own—

in them a dream of myself, my on-going-ness—
as if the future were caught in the outspread
web of my fingers. Their admirable length, their span

already a piano octave, seemed more than a child's,
mattered more than the silly girl in school
who questioned my color. When I held up my splayed hand,

light shone through the outline, pink skin
back-lit, just as the light lit each leaf,
the precise stems radiating outward from the branches

which surrounded the trunk. Exactly spaced,
they allowed only pieces of sky, the path of white buds
sensibly wound, not yet heady with scent

in the demanding heat. The day's fleshy blossoms unfastened
cupped petals large as dinner plates, their perfection
poised and unassailable. Just to touch them

meant a bruise, a yellow-brown shadow on the cream.
What I owned was the dim ground, the secret
pathways for ants and beetles. The line of roly-polies

turned their thin bodies into BB's, metal balls rolling away.
Molding the damp earth around my fist,
I still made houses for toads, a walled village.

Poison was everywhere: snakes, the oleander
lining the house, where black folks left us okra or peas,
a bushel of something, at night

when no one knew they came. But for the time being
I could still turn away. The tree,
another gorgeous southern thing, held me

from a longing so fierce I would go numb with it.
That world outside would claim me, close the self, lock it tight,
and what would it take to open again?

CATALPA

In dream, the wings
came out of nowhere, joined me to the birds'
swoop and dive above the sunken land.
I could see the rim of watermark around each tree—
in the one recurring flight, catalpa trees
and Genie Bell's house just beyond.

We collected worms from the ruts of trunks or as they hung
like stamens of the long white flowers the trees put out
each June. All around was the nasty smell
of last year's leaves crushed underfoot, but in my double life
she and I flew above all that, above the entire grove
planted for fishing bait. The pasty gutsy worms
loved by perch and bass, sold up on the corner.
The bait for her Sunday fish.

On the bogged edge of D'Arbonne Pond
filmed with greenest-green, where the bottom-eaters dozed,
I'd see her with the others, black faces
above the brimmed line of flowered dresses and hats,
bamboo poles arcing pale lines over the notched water. Quiet—
not like us on the manicured shore with our picnics and balls.
This scene is real, I think. Sometimes I confuse them,

the dream, that is, and the actual fishing.
I know the grove of catalpa trees from nights

I sort and piece. She bore me up on her wide body—
in that strange light she shone. We were safe up there,
I never doubted. I thought we shared some secret something
in my blood, in my slow white half-breed blood.

WANT

Every sign of the day flies white,
throws the pump bucket and water jug,
covers the saw and screech of making do.
I come back to paper scattered on sand, shutters banging,

and my young self still out there,
stumbling on the blowing beach,
high tide sucking her ankles
as she fights her way in a sideways gust.

I can't see through the storm
of so many years, and what can I do with her anyway?
Furious girl, daring it all
to get what she wants. So much wanting it's turned

indistinct, *silvery as the promise of torn clouds:*
As usual, she's all image and hyperbole. The hypnotic
sea foam churns up—what else?—beauty,
not the bitter brine of the hard water

slapped white. The fool in her
summoning Icarus caught up in pristine light,
and in the shattered sea, some miraculous
rising. She'll choke in the water's squall.

Midnight and my young self
will come dragging in, spent and bruised,
banging at the shack. The flimsy piece of driftwood
nailed to make a simple lever

                                will not hold the door.

WILLFUL

All day, I fought myself, every word
    invented to fit the seam of my gaze—
then fell asleep in late sun

that woke me, fur-mouthed and burned.
    I'm not ready for evening
in the bordering woods, my walk where bears prowl

through dusk. I chant my willful spell,
    Bears in the woods, Bears in the woods, Praise be,
Bears! I'm afraid they'll catch me anyway—

they look too much like stumps
    in the looming shade. Yesterday, I turned
to see the fisher's black flash cross my path.

Innards are all she eats: five house cats
    stolen for her litter just last week.
It's the closed summer dark

that sends me back to roadside light,
    where I name the easy *furled pods of milkweed /*
babies bound in fuzz...

And like a talisman, a thrush somewhere
    starts up: a moment made beautiful
by singing, and something else

starts dying. Flushed, nesting grouse
    scramble out in a rising tangle.
Struggle shakes the wall of leaves, the screen

of chlorophyll and spores, chemical cells,
    the on-going breathing air.
I can't look, hurrying up the road

to reach the field, expansive, benign,
    although it is nothing I want,
calling as it does to that cultivated thing, my heart.

ENVOY

The crows came back last night
in this, the blank center of October,
the broken line the lush world draws

to the hungry days of December.
Already they'll eat anything, craned neck
and squawk at the rag of flesh,

their beaks in every winter morning,
shrieking, ripping the profits from the jay's
torn craw. They serve themselves.

I'm not the first to hate their flapping
claim to the season, lured to the window
by their raw, gut-filled, strutting

common pride. Oh they bring out in me
the loftiest ideals, and see how I stumble,
falling back to the dog I gave away,

sour animal, who in the last moments
shook me with the wild sorrow
open in her comprehending face, pleading

clear as any speech: *don't leave me*
with these strangers. And I did,
I took that last look, and turned away.

DEATH OF PUZZLE

Grounded, the snow blinds—
sun-struck universe of slivers
aiming for the eye. Beyond, beyond:
the ginger cat's tuft of fur
swaying on a thorn. The glare
has picked it, the wind's dissection
inviting each cell to spin
its prism.
                    Inviting me, the one
who wishes *not* to see
what the fisher's appetite
accomplished in his killing
of the kitten. Why this

arrangement of molecules and time,
and why these words
fastening that surviving
light to the page
as clearly as the amber dimensions
of the fall wasp laced to the screen,
the particulate whole
defined by the frozen air?

MESSENGER

Throb of red, the cardinal
stutters through the trees' crossed-hatched
limbs, detail made present and aching
by the snow's work. I've wakened to a fairy tale
endlessness, a maze of lines
guarding the cardinals, who stitch and weave

a musical beat. All the varying whites
seem one in the air's held breath.
No sway, not one falling drift, polishes the light.
Just that rhythm I follow like a heart
back and forth, until something in me catches
a black shuffling at the woods' edge,
more hump than shadow, a dragged body.
It claims my eye before my eye can name it,
massive, indistinct, so much the shape of menace

in the corner of my sight, for a few seconds
I think I've called it, lured it out
from the vast resources of my dread.
But no, even as it disappears (into what?)
etched footprints show the path, saved by the snow
which has deceived me. And the birds cease.
All the blanketed morning, the birds cease.

SAME OLD

So much for burnt ends of toast, for turned milk
souring my coffee, the don't-mind-me-I'll-just-
eat-the-gizzard choked down at every meal; so much
for bleeding skin under the bitten-off nail,
sobbing only as the bath water ran, nibbling
through the afternoon to satisfy what nothing could.
I swallowed it all, my job

to take in trouble, shake out its little wings,
give it a place to sleep, as if grief were a truth
never before told, elevated to the status of vision,
or as I aged, wisdom, because don't we know
wisdom is learning to accept, etcetera, etcetera.
So much for that good girl, for guilt's
noose, and under it, the trapdoor and holding place,

should-haves piling up like leaves in October,
even that gold given the shivery spin of regret.
Oh the whole time I was taking a razor to everything,
cutting and shaping, refolding the same corners, making do,
the perennial teacher who couldn't give it a rest,
deprived mother of serve, serve, serve.
What soul could give its home to that love?

WHITE SEA

The color of emptiness and denial,
April's freeze
hardens again the melting field.

The balmy breath of last week's thaw
left rotting snow, a loose clutter of frostwork
my footsteps fall through.

Underneath, the layers are collapsing,
dismantling the readable strata,
the frozen stasis coming undone.

*

A warming of the surface and it goes smooth,
likens its sheen to feldspar,
glassy hard. But this morning,

a new inch of powder offers tracks, and as I follow,
I imagine the shudder of something just ahead,
wretched as hindsight.
                              The rabbit's footprints
trace the perimeter of the field, then disappear.
No sign of struggle, just a last print
in the circling white sea of snow.

*

New light hangs its curtain in the frosted window,
the feeder empties. Spring pushes in.
The Cape day shifts and flings,

wields its needled air—
going numb is the point of it.
The ocean underneath that wind is sapphire,

color of the killing cold, ice
riding the surface. In this white, perhaps
a poultice, a madstone to draw the poison out.

DISAPPEARANCES

Away from news of public bombs, private deaths,
away from grieving friends, I woke
to beach light, the water with no ripple to mar

its finish, no fissure or lip at the sand's edge,
just two surfaces in a thin kiss, drawing the line.
A flatness laid down, blue held to blue, continuing

past the breakwater. And the boat perched there,
static, as if it had no weight at all,
just the outline of a boat—the shell a child sees,

what he would draw on the rim of the water.
Underneath, nothing broke that wholeness
until I saw, on the bottom's quiet sand, somebody's shoe

resting on its side. Just another lost thing
in the list of wallets, watches, rings.
This one accidentally touching a nerve

should the right person see it
when the tide slips out,
the water doing what it does best—escaping.

AT BORIS'S ON THE OUTER BEACH

The tides are worthless,
though I pretend to read their comings and goings.
What use is the art of balance?

Shimmer distracts me, the great waste of shine
poured this way and that. In easy August,
I preen, my hair caught up in wind.

How could I grow old
when so much remains the same?
These days I weigh the beauty of this beach

against the weather's year-in, year-out
sculpting of the dunes, tearing away
the sand that holds the shack. The walls

loosen, scrabbling mice chew their way
through the famous wood, too near
my place in midnight's cracked bed—

the gnawing goes on till morning.
Nothing resists these hours and their law
of conflicting waters, which ride in,

take what they can, then vanish.
Summer flies to fall—
the white sea of everything will sweep us away.

II

LINDA'S POEM

We laughed in the snow. It was a blizzard
just starting to fall, but we didn't know.
We ran away like children—we were girls
really, too young for our young husbands,
and we teased, dinner growing cold on the table.
We broke the quiet furious snow
and stumbling in the thickening white,
shrieked and let ourselves fall
into each other's arms, her long falling
laugh in the snow's unwinding sheet.
Then we rose, brushing ourselves off, and walked
back toward the bright house, where she caught my arm,
stopping cold.
                    We were looking through a window
to another window across the room, and through that one
the glass of yet another, which found
the night-lit glittering snow on the other side.
Between those fixed layers, framed—the two men
sitting before the fire with their wine.
And later she wrote that as we paused
outside, it was as if we could see our lives waiting,
see the future as a separate and brief thing,
a glimpse of something fixed, unanswerable.
And she was sad when we went back inside,
having crossed a boundary.

AGAIN, AUTUMN

Under the misleading glitter of first snow,
every green's gone brittle in the seared
rattle of the trumpet vine, the grave-marking lily stalks,
and the annuals' blackened bodies
weep into the ground. It's a good excuse, isn't it,

the bearing down of the myth to show privation?
I work November's dirt in my hands,
obedient when the early dark sends me home.
When the girl left, the seasons fed
a single-minded vision, so convenient for her mother,

who could pin joy to spring, death to fall. Just as I
turn to elegy, interpreting the world's signs
in my favor—judgment on the crows, pity for the deer—
pushing the self to the center of all reason.

CALLED BACK

I.

The voice falters and the last thought
turns over like an empty shell, the words

hanging for an instant in the air.
The incoming tide, lapping

at letters someone's drawn, rides over
the little ridges of sand. The soul drifts forward,

stretches in the hammock of its being,
abeyance interrupted by the heart's stutter.

Then a pause, and in a rising
last beat, a flood pushes through the wide

channels of the arteries, the smaller
arterioles, the capillaries' tracing waterways,

all the dependencies towed under
in the swell and surge. The body is ruled

by thought and matter, carrying the unfathomable
soul this way and that. Buffeted,

cajoled by a lifetime's designs,
how could the soul not want this change,

the erasing of moment, hour, year, every sign
the body existed, its brief home

going under like that white strip out there
in the blue haze, the whole of non-being

calling it back.

II.

When she understood she'd entered another country,
crossed the chasm between illness and health,
well-being now forever on the other side—
recognizing at last that permanent separation
of *me* from *other,* the casual unconcern of those
who never have to consider their bodies—
when that day came, she boarded the New Year's late train
back to her childhood city, grateful she had strength

for the jerking, rocking local making its way from Penn Station
to New Haven, the usual transfer to the Boston line.
But this time when the electrical lines were cut,
no perfect dark but a dead silence in a black hour
until the stumbling pause and yank, the quick smell of hot steel
as the train lurched forward. The whole world seemed physical,
ever-moving, perpetual: no mystery
in the final divide. As there was none in the powerful drugs

she had courted, their invasion of a clot of cells.
Each battle was a reckoning for flesh, her past
I can beat this held forth, her flag, the war
cry of her will, as the chemicals blindly assaulted
everything good and bad in their path. The enemy
uncanny, her body something to negotiate: on-going
sores in her mouth, fire and brine in her gut.
Now she'd call a truce, she'd withdraw, return

to her brother waiting in Providence, the station's
faint salt air. He took her bag, always the same
desire to please her, his same sweetness,
though the gesture now seemed watchful, conscious, part of
her essential removal from the life of ordinary things.
She was not ordinary. The trip was not a whim.
The fact of dying took up every space, all her weight
belonged to it, all her self in its service.

She did not tell him what she knew from the doctor's call—
the obliging liver and kidneys captured
in their innate softness, the malignancies racing
first here then there. She had finished with that imagining.
She asked for a ride around the empty city, the two of them
following their childhood's map, school to school,
their father's hospital, the old house, reclaiming each place
as if to fix a history. Nothing seemed changed:

cold drizzle, steam rising from grates, the heater's
random click. All of it protecting them, their closeness
unassailable. They drove the dark familiar,
then redrove it, touching on each landmark
like the stops on a board game, replaying the round
as if they were small again, up too late after bedtime.
Until her silence said it was finished,
they could go to his home, his wife and children waiting.

This was her only goodbye, a storing up perhaps.
The cancer's malign outposts demanded a journey

she would not discuss. She gave no language to dying—
silence was her keeper, the law was pain, its body
lost to our news, our clocks. In the end
she lay unmoving, traveling
far beyond us in that room
where we kept waiting for her voice.

III.

We had to give permission.

All of us at the formal table,
    a good dinner, good wine. How we sat there

long afterward.   The bread we passed
    again, the wine. Talk and laughter,

the intercom on, reversed,
    so she could hear us, so she could know

we were safe,   that it was safe for her
    to leave us.

*

She came and went in flickers,
    time was the light

turned on, turned off.   For us
    the palliative day

allotting its tasks.
    Fifteen minutes to coax her socks

over the ruined skin,
    yellowed, strained, a palimpsest

for the bones beneath.
　　How she cried out

when we tried to lift her, how hard she tried
　　to be lifted.

*

Invariable grief note: *don't leave,*
　　don't leave.　　That wailing bird

chastened by her practice
　　leave-taking.　　Taking leave.

Abandoned syllable
　　on the tip of her tongue.

A blink, a breath
　　half-given to the air.

*

Between the sacred and the blank,
　　a short space.

We opened the doors, the windows
　　unlatched.　　We were careful

not to cry her back.

THE SEA CHEWS THINGS UP

When I woke, the waves had gone black,
turning over the macerated
curd of the ocean bottom, heaving its sludge
onto the beach. Some storm far out, I thought,
had ravaged the sea, stirred up its bed,
sent the whole mess flying to shore.
At my feet I found a grave of starfish,
broken and gnarled among the fleshy
spines and heads. Every shade of death
covered the sand. It looked hopeless
in the pale day but for the birds,
a congress of gulls, terns, and the rarest plovers,
calm for once, satiated, a measure of
the one law: this sea will claim it all—
feed them, catch them, grind their complicated bones.

THE RELEASE

I.

I lose myself in all the falling
leafy light, gold-on-gold
bartering through the afternoon.
How many leaves will it take
to fill this pond, where thousands float,
feathery, slight, gilding
the surface. The water has settled
into clarity, all its complication
brooding on the bottom, reminding me

of Linda near the end. She waited
as if waiting were the reason for it all,
oblivious to the bedside comings and goings.
Flickering with morphine, the face we knew
receded. She was feeding a great privacy,
moving past the years she once said
were fixed with our names;
moving past the self's accumulation
to the very point of spirit, dot
in the web binding our lives to hers,
drawn in and borne away.

The sky goes flat, and all the forest
racket suspends. Bruised reds

interrupt the golds. I see the bird reflected
before I see the bird himself: the unfolding
heron's blue clockwork.
The water gives a quiver of disorder,
no more than a pause in a string of words.
A wasp lumbers in the air
with no screen to beat against.

II.

The field has been waiting all this time
  to offer up its green to bristle and bur,

the raspy wires hooking my ankle.
  I've needed to see these crossed grasses

flung by the mower, the nested feathers
  she could name. She knew every cricket and cicada

crowding the air. Doesn't that universe of keening
  make September a grieving thing? But as I reach

the trees' blind opening, a deer
  flies at me, wild-faced, the raised body

hurling itself forward, hooves
  veering as I freeze. And just like that, she's gone—

Linda, who I can't keep,
  even the rising trill of her laugh

already revised, reordered.
  The weather bears down.

I'm turned by the rush of sudden birds,
  a fan opening.

III.

We'll call this dying: the soul
fumbles out of the dark room into the darker
hallway, almost feeling its way as it separates
from the body's time and space.
It has to regain itself, this soul, its definition
caught as it has been for so long
in the body on the bed. The gorgeous quiet
has already descended, no hum or tick
or expectant sleep of a soul deeply tuned.
Maybe someone sobs, the guest
holds back, or the one
loved beyond all estimation still
holds the weighted hand. Or it is 3 a.m.
and whoever has lain beside the dying
all night with the work of waiting
walks out in pajamas into the black wet grass...
But never mind, here's the moment,
almost with the last heartbeat: the soul
is stretching, hesitating forward,
a second of air, a brief exhalation of nothing,
more the shiver a little breath makes.
Then the pause in which something
is thinking itself forward
toward a distant twin, maybe a line of light
under the door that leads through the house
then out into the night. Out to the celestial
shimmer that belongs to the earthly moon,

that appropriated body we believe
informs our own. And to the surrounding
kin of stars, star from dying star
passing on its dust, every physicality connected
to another in that transforming that keeps making
something of itself over and over again—yes, well,
imagine joy, as the soul gives it all
a brief nod and flies on past.

WHITE MORNING

How could it be so ruined, the woods
ravished by a grainy sleet, a gravelly white
sodden leaves and limbs poke through.
I have lost my killer instinct
for beauty, for embellishing and relishing
the art of it. No lacework to imagine
here: the spoiled autumn
dies into slush, and the deer who roamed free
yesterday, the thrill of my gaze locking theirs,
have quit the neighborhood. Not one captured thing
to trade, though I look hard
first one way into the wasted repetition,
then the other, but no, I cannot
coax a quarrel out of this unforgiving ground.

YOU MUST CROSS THE BLACK RIVER

If only is your governing rule,
each day's measuring stick held out
to find the lack, the thwart, the missing
you continue to mourn.

Poor heart, with its struggle and stutter,
its fat blue beating. And how could you
forget it—listening all night, head on your arm.
That voice in a knocking house

has nothing to do with the soul, what you call
unquenchable, bloodless
in the sweep of white. You break open the fruit,
the mass of swollen seeds, each its own

fiery globe, a ruby-flicker in the nested
chambers of pale flesh, for a glimpse
of *what-passes*. But even this holds you
to the physical, the mapped, and you must leave all that:

you must cross the black river
and take up the laws of nothingness and waiting.
She'll come, the one dressed cold and still
in a clamor of light.

III

IN WOODS

Blind, I was nowhere inside,
drawn past the verge of woods
in the fallen night, blank
haze hanging
a hand over my eyes.
Blind night, no moon
white as a shout, a startled
shake to keep me
out of woods—no owl this time
sweeping before me. Fall's quiet
old now: the waving leaves, the fine
flying needles of the pines
dead and given to ground.
Every outline had filled in,
paid back its black
refusal, and I almost didn't see.
I was walking the silencing woods
when wildness woke, took hold
to turn me, something far and fast
lit the dark way back.

CANE

When the mule balked, he hit him
sometimes with the flat of a hand
upside the head; more often
the stick he carried did its angry trick.
The mule's job was to power the press,
iron on iron that wrung the sugar
out of cane, circling under the coarse
beam attached to his shoulders and neck.
That mule of my childhood
was black, remained blackly obedient
as round and round he made himself
the splintered hand of a clock, the groan
and squeak of machinery chewing
the reedy stalks to pulp, each second
delivering another sweet thin drop
into the black pot at the center.

He hit him with a rag, old headrag,
but the animal winced only with the thrash
of a cane stalk itself—he squinted
under the rule of that bamboo.
The sun was another caning
on his black-hot flesh. He was slow
as the blackstrap syrup the boiled sugar made,
so true to the circle he dragged
we hardly saw him. We loved the rustling

house of green cane, blind in that field
of tropical grasses whose white plumes
announced the long season's wait.
We yearned for the six-foot stem, the eventual
six pieces the machete sliced
at the joints, then the woody exterior
peeled back lengthwise with a blade.
It was a black hand we waited for, his job
to lay bare the grainy fiber we chewed.
That juice on our tongues
was his sweetness at work.
Chester was his name, he kept the mule.

BURIAL

Later he died, and it was then I think
I began to give sense to every motion
I had not heeded. Already I could no longer
kill an ant, a wasp, without some smallness
setting in: the burden of my own hunger
apparent in every living thing. But that was after

Chester buried the dog, after he walked us down
into the swampy woods. Sunday morning, already October,
the grasses shot through with yellow, the locust
bearing its alligator bark. So early
we were in our nightgowns, my sister and I,
my brother trailing. The durable creatures of the air

zoomed and crossed, my heart lit with grief
for the dog, my own dear fierce animal
mysteriously dead, firing the rage which would lead me,
while Chester shouldered the dog on one side, the shovel
like a rifle on the other, come once again
as a favor to my mother, who had no man for this weight.

And the new sun faced us, flat across the flat land,
making its way across his quiet face
as he dug the hole. My sister sobbed, my brother watched,
and I was so busy in my head, even now

I can see only the lovely patterned fur
arranged in the hollow of red dirt. Not Chester,

who was one more thing in the landscape, his presence
something I took in like air. Not his glistening
onyx self, his color smooth as mineral, or the comfort
of the low voice giving a few words in praise of dog,
although I heard him take one deep breath,
the *amen,* when he finally rested.

JANUARY

Each flake was like a person, Miss Mary Wilson said.
She could have made it all up, beloved teacher

with her talk of those intricate, myriad
inhabitants of the air. Now in a winter made of snows

I know what she tried to teach
in the sleet and blowing bits or the motionless falling

of fairy tale flakes we imagined big as hands.
She meant us to dream

beyond shape—the point was to see
what couldn't be seen. Their patterns stunned us

as we cut to her approving eye. She wanted all of physics
to intervene, science blessing us

with a model of space shining in each speck,
determined by the essential

crystal at the center. She granted this privilege,
while outside, robins dug into the ever-green

St. Augustine grass, the Jerusalem cherry set its fruit.
She pasted pages of snowflakes on the windows,

and the north loomed, a vast impenetrable white
waking in me my own unknowable germ—

the hint I catch on my tongue,
fleeing before shape can coax it whole.

AT FOURTEEN

What I'd never seen in the bayou's dank greens:
a diving pelican below the surface, neck twisted
to throw back its head, mouth wide.
I saw the live fish flap into the sack,
the wings flail at the water's capture
before they dragged back into air.
And this was just the bay, not the burning
noon-day white on white, the white
water riding the blue. And the noise of it
nothing could stop. No picture
showed that sound, the on and on
revealing and taking back. Even the color
was all sensation, gleaned from the motion
of one thing being changed into another:
semi-dead, dead, rotting, and rotten,
a stew of debris in the pockets of air.

So the roar of it overtook me, my desire
brought to the surface for once, the tide load at my feet
shoving and crashing, too cold, too salty,
out of nowhere the wind lifting the sand
in a stinging sheet, ripping the waters
which could snap my backbone in half.
As it could now, years after: the networking
fin and jaw, fledgling birds dragged under, the bluefish's
snap, the gull scream

guarding a graveyard of shells. In and out,
back and forth, the rocking on white sand, black sand.

THE OLD QUESTION

What will it take to let myself speak?
June is a chorus of blues, delphiniums
rioting at the gate, the pressing
summer air. On the deck, lemon birds
quick as poppyseed chime
and spring into the morning blaze.
It's too clean, too clear, this weather

set against my fear. Cornered,
the old question screeches and dives.
Tell the truth, I think, and what is that
but a creature with claws?
I bite my lip, remembering
last evening's walk at the deep end of dusk
when everything had shut itself up
but the one yellow-eyed, secretive thrush—
silver call in the night.

SPEECH TO THE SELF

People have been dying and you
are lying on the beach. You're lying here
listening to the world
inside: no, it's the soul in you,
and you want enough room to hear.
You lay down your bushy head with all that gray
flying out on the damp sand.
You let your head be its own weight, a rock
among all the other rocks on the stony
two or three feet of tide line—
the fertile wrack of it
made from dead things
and the miniscule cells they feed.

You fish for it, the tiny tail of a moment,
the trail end of a thought, a listening
you've ignored all this time. You think
I could make something with that, and
in that *maybe,* all possibility in you
becomes very still, your body
inert on the sand. Because all the dead ones
are living there too, guests
in the shell of a thought, and if it were real,
this shell would be a spiral shape,
a moonsnail—oh but why bring the moon into it?
What did the moon ever do for you,

that preoccupied mother
nursing her schedule, half-here, flirting
half-light through mists and trees and buildings.
The soul doesn't want her moody truth.
Try on death for truth: the incomparable
here now, gone tomorrow.

Was it grief that sent your soul away?
To what secret room, through which stubborn door?
On the other side, she's inching her way out,
uncurling with the loosened thought,
murmuring in a breath. And you want
just to pull her out of there,
give her your voice box, like a toy,
a puzzle, the child in her
turning it over and over, putting it to her ear,
her small fingers probing in the flat light
until satisfied, she wakes to your waiting—
she has something to say.

STANLEY AND ELISE

His step tentative on the stones,
he inches his way forward. Deafness has deepened
his abstracted look, but summer saves him,

brings admirers to the garden's
Rose of Sharon trees. Elise hovers,
bent under the ghostly blues

guarding the door. Her hands worry the bright
silk of her blouse; her mind wants to fly.
When I try to bring her back

to the Provincetown of paintings and friends,
she shakes her floating hair and goes back calling
Stanley, Stanley.... He won't stop digging in the dirt.

His pleasure is in the pairing of opposites:
flowers arranged in tiers, each hue
with its response, each tier rising to answer

the previous progress of blooms. It's a lesson
I take back to the dunes, the shack
where I'm reading St. Augustine, the old quarrel

about the *inquieta,* the heart's heedless rush and stutter.
My soul, says Elise, *is tired of me.* Stanley's heart
is in the garden. Nighttime for him argues open

the seeds of doubt, writing in his little room.
It's all a contradiction, the interwoven dark
rising and falling as the oil lamp flares and smokes.

I lay the book aside, take the chimney from its base
to wash it. My bony hand folds in,
fingertips against the layer of greasy carbon,

sliding it off in pieces—
as if the black were wearing the glass,
a filmy night thing falling to specks, black stars

in the good water. My knuckles push against
the bowed middle, where light shines brightest,
the part that says *if I break, here's where.*

STANLEY'S FIRST DEATH

1.

The body became a vessel, the rasping breath
its proof, and before him nothing
but that ocean sweep
he traveled over. His spirit
lofted forth, his voice
a long quavering
when the wind permitted, as if
out there somewhere some god
held the string.

He was carried somewhere else, who knows?
then fell back, found
the diligent old body at his desk.

2.

What wind blew in this long-winged
sylvan creature to flirt with the page?
Rising dot, it punctuates and rests
long enough to be forgotten: no noisy
moth at the light or the hovering
network of a dragonfly.
A mote of sorts—floater in my aging eye.
Catch it in late fall, half lit
as faint snow, melting as it touches.

YOU WOULDN'T SAY GOODBYE,

so now you come back as both substance
and shadow. You aren't even a woman now,
the soul beyond female and male, or something
comprising the two. But I'm bound
by human image. I look into the sea
and only find myself, the same me, limited to flourish and sweep.
I want to see you again, the woman-you,
the one I spoke to here in letters, and you held on to them
for your husband to return afterward, their messages
turned back on their owner with the indifference of mirrors.

You who wouldn't speak of dying,
what am I to think—that love was enough?
The understood as plain
as this ocean stretching before me, or the mote I ignore
floating in front of everything I see?
The sacred is one step away from the profane,
you said that once, as if I'd asked the question.
There's no answer out there in the miles of choppy water,
not one white wave to follow in. But the eye
is never what it seems, its matter separate
and distinct, the cornea a transparent rigid shell,
while the body languishes in its ropy
strands of tissue, entirely perishable.

62

DEATH OF A GULL

Worse than his pain was his acceptance,
the wing loosely dragging beside him
while he did his best not to notice. As if the impossibility
might drop away, he ambled, a hen's shuffle
from oceanside toward the plovers' nesting ground,
but the little birds came diving, driving him back.
Beak open, he hissed like a swan, his only show.
Another gull glided down, just one—perhaps his mate—
companions side by side until he ignored
the cues for flight. She spiraled out of the path
of passersby, but he only turned his head away,
like a toddler's shy aside, to make the intruder disappear.

Day and night turned over, the waves
close then far. The weight dangling at his side
grew heavier and he learned to fix his eye
on the middle distance. Alone and offered up,
he roosted there, suffering the tide-rich sand
and the roving metal-throated birds
from which he once stole fish. The spewing waves,
the crabs awash, haphazard heads and claws,
offered nothing he wanted to eat.
The whole thing reeked. Overhead, the hypnotic
sequined blue glittered and teased.

The green sea went about its business,
sifting, hooking, grinding. Bottom waters
boiled and rose, feeding all the frenzied
multiplying cells, which brought the little fish,
the bigger fish, and then the seal,
whose lackadaisical tossing off of bones
made him the birds' life of the party.
The crippled gull heard them all, but as if
he lived in another country. There was nothing
but the square of sand he squatted on.
Flying was a prick of recognition gone foreign,
then a nagging absence, swallowed up by the wind.
Hour by hour, he became that emptiness,
just a breathing thing on the moving sand.
And then the line dividing the pulse
from the intake of air,
air ruffling feathers he no longer felt.

MOONSNAIL

I killed it for its shell, its design and shape,
not caring about the animal coiled inside, faceless
mudworm, intestinal, with its amorphous foot
fixed like a door to repel crabs or gulls.
I thought I'd see some taut muscle, not that oozing,
the giving over of a thick pulsing jelly
wound and wound to its end. I didn't think of it
answering to a clock, hurling forward as the waves

shoved onto sand, waiting to open and burrow,
to feed before the water dragged it back.
Traffic of the tides, that ugly life
filled a house which took on hues of blue and rose,
some pretty moss as it aged, perfect form
spiraling to the innermost point
marked by a round black eye.

Five shells now, lined up by size,
but not like Russian dolls, an amusing emptiness
to fit a pattern. These are freed from their true selves—
the disgusting, the lax—though I admit, not evil,
not what my grandmother warned against: the devil
waiting for the opening praise provides.
Spit, she said, in the face of beauty or truth
to chase harm away.

                         It's useless to spit in this ocean,

always the churning surface and everything underneath
riding in. Polished by the sea's punishing thrust,
empty shells survive. But I didn't want those—
I chose the inhabited, the *something there,*
and removed it. It's simple: I laid each one out
in the blinding day, the sun did its work, the ants came,
then I shook it hard.

PRAISE HIM

Dog whose middle name is *do good,*
whose sigh is the birth of patience; dog
whose middle name is angel, offering
the blessing of his lick, his weight as guide.
Carrying is what he does best, and so he does

love the stuffed bear we call Baby and all the risk
of teeth in fur, our captured hands as we grab
the sticks of the world, where he turns
his desire to even the inferior, insignificant
breaking ones. He holds them all, as he tries

to hold the low wind's message in his upheld nose.
He holds himself as guard, ears pricked
for the snow's command. Ice-crystals in his lashes,
eyes narrowing at the moon traveling under the cloud,
he'll burrow into the snow if it's too cold,

just as he finds the girl's side when she cries,
leaning his body against hers, finding
her eyes to hold, his the eyes of the ever-present
mother, the language of *now* in his hungry tongue.
He knows with what degree of whine to shade

his answering bark; has learned to soften it
to a vowel when she questions, though finally

he must lie down with the secrets he carries,
heaving his weight aside, cornered in the one life
of the dumb, the never-to-speak, full with knowing.

THE HERRING RUN

1.

Din at noon, wind and glare
and three small cousins I've brought to see the herring
make their ancient run back to the sea.
They hardly hear me and what's the use—they don't want
my sort of lesson in mystery and gratitude.
Fish drum the water, a thrashing mass in the two-mile fall
from the pond where they've left their floating
webs of spawn. The boys beg for nets,
jumping the jutting rocks and laddered bridges
the endless fish plummet down.
Out on her ledge, the one girl taunts the boys:
she's going to dive right in, her piercing yell
let loose on their limits.

2.

The ocean riled-up, frothing, she's wild
up and down the sea-swept beach, collecting
stray crab parts in a broken cardboard box.
April's sea brings up its bleached, salt-eaten
whites. Some hooked interlocking
legs and claws still movable, correct—
she'll take them home, she says: somewhere in there
is enough to make a whole crab.

You can't do that, scream the boys,
but she shakes them loose, shakes her sleek black head.

STANLEY'S GOODBYE

Farewell! he cries, arms thrown wide, taking in
from his fixed chair the garden's ever-changing
terraced walls. The color now full and fiery
as August will allow, he's content to sit there,
planted where the layers begin
on the bottom tier, and there before him
all the lovelinesses, the visitors, the half-lit
hanging slip of moon. Late afternoon
and his sudden voice proclaims

like the bell in the ancient country's ancient town,
walled hilltop face of ruin, where the saved church
still looks down on the continuing sky
of Constantine's great harbor. And when the bell
eclipses the silence, ringing out,
you first think it triumphant, but then
it pulls you back, jarring you
with its complication, summoning
from a place you've never been.

LISTEN, SPIRIT

I didn't go around talking to you. I believed
in prayer, that necklace of psalms, and failing that,
the willow's arches above my head. In those fans and fronds

I thought I could see it all—the past
like a distant winter, the future... well, the leaves
hung before my face, and I could not imagine

beyond them. I needed signs, I see that now:
baby squirrels born in the woodstove, then
their mother dead in the road. The children

cradled the tiny beings in their palms, nursing with eyedroppers,
a finger massaging the belly that had just been fed.
I saw you as another mother, hovering.

But you are not the sentimental one,
you don't consider permanence, and you don't care
about my American happiness. So easy to confuse you

with cozy self-regard, conjure up some awareness
wanting me to winnow out life's meaning.
I admit—I've been in love with appearances,

the ruthless sea, the toad's gazing eye. Year after year
believing it was the same toad in my garden! The transmigration
of one spirit into another!

Charmed by shine,
I've dragged a finger through the flame and stared into the sun.
Imagine, thinking that's where I'd see you.

AT HOME

Now when I find the fuchsia's swollen fruit,
the dark pods tender and bleeding, so many
hidden under the leaves after their blossoms fell,
knowing I didn't see them—my job
to find the tight green buttons when it matters,
snap them for the good of the plant—

and when I consider the fruit fly,
little bad-winged sucking thing—hovering
over the peaches, riding the damp air—
which slides between my clapping palms
and shimmies through the dishcloth's slap,
I think I have not understood decay

or the seed at the heart of it.
Why else would it live in all ripe things,
not an error, lured or invading,
but waiting there like weather on the verge,
at home in the landscape, which for now
glosses over the laden stillness before fall.

Even my clean kitchen, supplied
with every manner of spice and staple,
is full of dying. I am faced with limits:
the berries at their fullest

just skirt the edge of rot, the fig splits
at my touch, the bruising flesh-to-flesh.

And though I set the sharpest knife between us,
the rosy wound patterns
the last burst of sunset, the shades of red
I travel to the ocean to see, where even now
I want to turn away—all of it
deadly and delicious in my eyes, my mouth.

VULTURE, CIRCLING

February white, and the clean wing
of the vulture punctuates
the pristine air, the snow so lit
it's blue, another sea, a heaven for grief.
But this bird knows what the dead are for,
knows what's ripe to be taken,
his serrated feather-edge like a saw
working the sky's perimeter. His life
is bent on watching, waiting
for the second to sweep
his sleek body down. For him, accuracy
is what I call ferocity. I'm the one
assigning value, my warning in the word.
Vulture, turkey buzzard, crow—all of them
repel me with their unflinching need.
The body dies, they eat it,
rot and all, a progression
not so different from the ordinarily beautiful
flower giving itself up to fruit, then the fruit
withering for the sake of seed.
And so on, without sentiment.

SOUL

It is not the angel riding a goat,
trying to make him go. It does no work
with refusal or guilt, which loves
only its contorted self. But fancies instead
my terrier's long pink tongue,
how it teases out the bone's marrow,
tasting with all its muscle.

The angel is silver, but so is the goat
and the box on which they perch,
a Victorian gesture in the mansion
where I spent the fall. They have followed
me home, their permanent shine presuming,
while around me, everything withered,
slowly froze, and began its turn
toward white. The snow
is nothing but a great emptiness,
and I'm tired of trying to find a secret there.
But look—one leaf
skittering across the glazed surface
catches its stem to stand upright,
the shape of a hand waving.

"You Must Cross the Black River": The line "You must cross the black river" is taken from David Ferry's poem "In the Reading Room," which reads "The page is blank until the mind that reads / crosses the black river...."

"The Sea Chews Things Up": This poem owes a debt to Alan Dugan's "The Sea Grinds Things Up," and is dedicated to him.

"Salt" is for Sara Warner-Phillips.

"Called Back" is for Robert Corrente.

"The Release" is for Star Lawrence.

"Burial" is for my sister Maria.

"The Herring Run" is for Hannah Elizabeth Phillips.

Ted Rosenberg

CLEOPATRA MATHIS was born and raised in Ruston, Louisiana. Her first five books of poems were published by Sheep Meadow Press, and are distributed by University Press of New England. Her most recent book, *What to Tip the Boatman?*, won the Jane Kenyon Award for Outstanding Book of Poems in 2001. She has received two National Endowment for the Arts grants, in 1984 and 2003; the Peter I.B. Lavan Younger Poets Award from the Academy of American Poets; a Pushcart Prize; the Robert Frost Award; a 1981–82 Fellowship in Poetry at the Fine Arts Work Center in Provincetown; The May Sarton Award; and Individual Artist Fellowships in Poetry from both the New Hampshire State Council on the Arts and the New Jersey State Arts Council. Since 1982, Cleopatra Mathis has been Professor of English and Creative Writing at Dartmouth College, where she directs the creative writing program. She lives with her family in Hanover, New Hampshire.